Borderland

ALSO BY JULIE R. DARGIS

Seven Sonnets
Pit Stop in the Paris of Africa
Reader's Guide: Pit Stop in the Paris of Africa
White Moon in a Powder Blue Sky

Borderland

An Exploration of States of Consciousness
in New and Selected Sonnets

Julie R. Dargis

HERMES HOUSE PRESS

Copyright © 2018 by Julie R. Dargis
All rights reserved. No part of this publication may be used in any manner whatsoever without the written permission of the author, except for the inclusion of brief quotations contained in critical articles or reviews.

For inquires, contact the author at:
www.juliedargis.com

Published by Hermes House Press
San Juan Capistrano, California
www.hermeshousepress.com

Design by Jules Hermes, Hermes Creative
www.hermescreative.net

ISBN: 978-0-9912614-5-1

To my brother, and all who share a love for learning.

CONTENTS

Acknowledgments
ix

Preface
xiii

Part One: Nature's Bounty
1

Part Two: The Art of War
15

Part Three: The Science of Illusion
23

Part Four: Zero to Infinity
37

Epilogue: Sonnet Cycle of the Seven Chakras
47

About the Author
57

Endnotes
59

Further Reading
61

ACKNOWLEDGMENTS

In addition to the many scholarly papers I have written as a PhD student at the California Institute for Human Science over the past two years, I have continued to explore my studies through poetry. During this time, many members of the CIHS community have supported me. I am indebted to Dr. Hope Umansky, Dean of CIHS; Dr. Thomas Brophy, the Executive Dean and my advisor; and Dr. Ji Hyang Padma for their continuing support. To Federico Miraglia, with whom I started my program, thank you for your keen insights and unyielding encouragement. To Victoria Barnhill, Anna Gallich, Kristi Inzunza, Kelley Spence, and John St. Claire, who share my path and continue to inspire me along the way, I offer my gratitude.

Some of the work included in this volume has been previously published by Indie House Press. "Liquid Stone" appeared in *Seven Sonnets* (2012). "After the Conflict Before the Peace," "Blind Return," "Christ Age Prague Spring," "Thy Neighbor's Heart," "The Likes of Me," "The Promise of Peace," and "Silent Music" are included in *Pit Stop in the Paris of Africa* (2013). "Bach Flower Power," "Falling to Grace," "Fight or Flight," "Future Perfect," "Fun with Physics," "If Midnight were Noon," "Radio Flyer," "Spirit Animal," "Sung by the Moon," "Surrender to Gaia," "The Great Halls of Science," "The Power of Choice," "The Shadow of Power," "When Spirit Calls," and "White Light" are included in *White Moon in a Powder Blue Sky* (2016).

One does not become enlightened by imagining figures of light, but by making the darkness conscious.

--C. G. Jung

Before the advent of relativity, physics recognized two conservation laws, the law of the conservation of energy and the law of the conservation of mass. By means of the theory they have been united into one.

--A. Einstein
Relativity: The Special & General Theory
100th Anniversary Edition

PREFACE

Poetry, when taken in as a single breath, connects us to the lungs of a greater consciousness. It has the power to illuminate as easily as it brings us face to face with the shadow sides of ourselves—and others.

Taken as a whole, poetry can cut across space and time, as can be found in the words of William Blake:

> *To see a world in a grain of sand*
> *And heaven in a wild flower,*
> *Hold infinity in the palm of your hand*
> *And eternity in an hour.*

In the section on "Nature's Bounty," I share the simplicity and pureness of nature that has inspired me. This is some of my newest work, spawned from a sense of safety, security, and healing.

Prior to settling in Southern California to write and study, I had worked intensely in many countries around the world where conflict or natural disasters shrouded the day-to-day reality. This resulted in the accumulation of some deep-seated trauma.

When seeking to heal trauma, one may think that the root cause of the pain has been resolved, only to find that there is often a depth to healing that continues on an emotional level well after the initial intervention. In this way, the realm of subtle energy medicine is similar to modern-day medicine since healing in either of these worlds, although seemingly magical at times, is a process.

Through verse, contemporary poet Ed Bok Lee elegantly captures the realities of trauma. In his work, "Whorled," Lee conveys the depth of his own suffering as one in a long line of spiritual refugees. His prose, reflected in the lives of his immigrant neighbors, outlines a shared pathway to healing.

In the section, "The Art of War," the darker confines of consciousness are investigated. In much of this work, I suggest that if one walks through the darkness, one comes to find that life itself is the light.

British biologist and philosopher, Rupert Sheldrake, has written in "Science Set Free" that there are ten dogmas of modern science. The first two dogmas include the beliefs that science is essentially mechanical, and all matter is unconscious.

Sheldrake implied that the experimentation currently delving into states of consciousness has yet to statistically quantify and replicate discoveries within mainstream science.

Dr. Hiroshi Motoyama, the founder of the California Institute for Human Science, specified that the reason it is so difficult for scientists to incorporate subtle energies into experimentation is because physical devices are only able to measure physical phenomenon.

A new paradigm in the discovery of the nature of reality is needed for the subtle sciences so that they may be admitted more readily into the halls of science. The premise is simple: Making a wider array of approaches to healing more accessible in one's quest for wellness increases one's healing options. The section, "The Science of Illusion," contemplates the role that consciousness plays in the pursuit of scientific understanding. As it relates to consciousness, Dr. Motoyama offers:

> *Non-sensory states of consciousness do exist, but we need to know more about the specific mechanism involved, not only to add to the general store of knowledge, but to help individuals who desire to explore the potential forms of consciousness which lie within themselves.*[1]

Beyond our own atmosphere on earth lies the wonders of the cosmos. Within even further dimensions, the laws of nature as we know them tend to dissolve. Space and time take on new qualities as the interplay between physics and spirituality continues to stretch our minds.

In the Buddhist tradition, for example, conventional truth is not denied. Rather, science is embraced as a means to understand the world around us. Still, there is more. When discussing the juxtaposition between religion and the laws of science, Buddhist monk and philosopher, Matthieu Ricard, states that Buddhism:

> *Quite simply affirms that, if we dig deep enough, there is a difference between the way we see the world and the way it really is, and the way it really is, we've discovered, is devoid of intrinsic existence.*[2]

The sonnets in "Zero to Infinity" ponder how rays of light in the natural world, as well as light that can be found in the cosmos and beyond, contribute to states of consciousness. This section also considers where humankind lands on the spectrum relative to infinity.

In the Epilogue, "Sonnet Cycle of the Seven Chakras," I turn to the eastern Vedic tradition to reflect upon the progression of life through the lens of the chakra system. This work attempts to move beyond color, sound and the physiological linkages to these energy centers in order to arrive at the heart of the matter: *the connection of our physical bodies to our subtle minds.*

The exploration of states of consciousness leads one into many areas of study. My work with consciousness has touched on topics such as: (a) healing and the subtle body; (b) intuition and the soul; (c) physics and the nature of reality; and (d) the afterlife and near-death experiences. Many of the sonnets in this volume use these areas of study to contemplate consciousness. For readers who would like to delve more deeply into these subjects, a list of books is provided in the section on "Further Reading."

The beauty of poetry lies not in its words, but the music that vibrates within them. To explore states of consciousness is to seek beauty. To find beauty is to merge with light.

Julie R. Dargis
Carlsbad, CA
February 2018

PART ONE
Nature's Bounty

Borderland

Rosa was covered in dew. The dampness
Weighed heavily upon her. Like fog, it
Would lift. Above the crest, a patch of clouds
Gained ground as the moon rolled into the sun.
Suspended in twilight, Rosa rested
Quietly in a world without borders.
Between states of consciousness. Borderland.
Navigation required that she be her
Own witness. Rosa thought this apropos.
Nature still had much to teach her, she mused.
She rose into the coolness surrounding
Her, sparking an insatiable thirst.
As her roots dug deeply into the soil,
Glad for the breeze, she reached out to the light.

Bach Flower Power

I dig in around the roots of the white
Rose bush, clearing away dead, fallen leaves.
I offer them to the wind. Dark blotches
On yellowed wings flitter in spirals as
They make their way downward. The next day the
Nose of a dog nuzzles them back into
The earth. The roots of wellness forever
Imprinted on fields of energy, I,
Too, have savored flora's transmutation.
Two drops, three times a day, transported on
Ether the essence to heal. Returning
The favor, I add two drops of the Bach
Remedy to the watering can, tilt
It over the bush and douse the petals.

Sung by the Moon

Under the green-grey haze, the sun was still.
A pelican slid by, its husky wings
Trailing a crusted beak. Dozens of boards
Paddled toward an impending swell beyond
The horizon. Lateral cliffs lay down
Upon the ocean floor as the tide—a
Hologram of shimmering rock—splashed in
Glittering white light under the small feet
Of children. Harmonious half-notes stacked
In thirds on the warm-cool breeze of winter.
A full moon reflected the foamy spray,
Music of an end-of-year-lullaby.
Sung by the still, small voice of breaking waves,
The sound of silence poured onto the beach.

Liquid Stone

Molten lava, liquid stone release your
Heart from the matter at hand, from the pain
Of stillness, from the pleasure of past lives.
You are not dead at all. Only you know
To coax a pond in spring without remorse
As it trickles over your back, your sides,
Warming you, cooling you, passing you by.
Only you know of the past particles—
Story rough lava domes—burning, ablaze,
Carried away in your wake upon wings
Of shear hydrogen, one and then two breaths
Taken in as they expand, flow. Void of
Alter excrement. Yes, I have said it.
Rolling thunder, I know you are alive.

Winter Solstice

A feather stretches across the sky toward
Sunrise—a ball of velvet light, bursting
In tone and tenor. The promise of a
New day disbands, blinding the eyes of the
Hawk. The briskness dissipates on thin air
As the hawk soars in dreamless sleep. A cloud
Of meta-reality within sight,
The whole of its body plunges to earth.
In broad daylight, the observer becomes
The observed. As morning lengthens, the hawk
Awakens to wondrous slumber. Beyond
The vista, within the depths of winter,
Solstice transmutes its wings to bone. As
The clutch of night wanes, somnambulists rise.

"Shivo Hum"

Worlds collide under the surface. The depth
Of a channel, the length of a lifetime.
Until, reaching my hand upward, the sun
Glints off the tips of my fingers as they
Emerge. Against the resistance, I pull
Myself out of the water. Leaving the
Half-moons that slice through the dug-out behind.
Falling into the light, I am made whole.
Cross-legged, earth gathers under me in
A mesh of time. As I rise, the netting
Flows through me with the lucidity of
A jellyfish. Astounded, I fall back
To earth, a witness to the weightlessness.
The joy of transcendence, swimming in light.

Surrender to Gaia

Inhale. We begin in Child's Pose, arms stretched
Out. Heels back, hands square. Downward facing dog.
I turn my head to track the passing breeze.
My eyes lock onto the rustling palm fronds.
Exhale. Return to all fours. Cat-Cow. Five
At your own pace. In the pool, waves pop to
The surface in nickel-sized swirls, twisting
As they reach back in time. Stand with your hands
To your heart. Breathe. Arms up, lean back. Micro-
Backbend. Fold forward. Cradle your elbows.
Lie down, head back, legs up. Fish pose. Release.
Surrender to Gaia. My arms and legs
Flop out. Savasana. My heart takes a
Bow as my mind flashes indigo blue.

Spirit Animal

Soft and subtle the rattling shakes as
My mind drops under the world. Before me
A swirl of color gives way to a wide
Array of animals. A pack of wolves,
The wings of a hawk, the belly of a
Hippo. The silver tail of a sly red
Fox darts about, chasing them all away.
For it is he who is mine. He circles
The stones of a fire pit, creating a
Sacred space. I enter on the skin of
Deer moccasins. The beating of drums pulls
My feet into the clay-like earth in a
Ceremonial dance. I am the fox,
We are the fire, rising in flames of smoke.

Nature's Munitions

At the height of vibration, instructing
Us toward love of self, compassion trumpets
Inner revolution. Bacteria,
Boots on the ground, combine naval reserves
Of DNA, deployed at five percent.
Nature's munitions unfurl the fruits of
The earth. Circling the foods that we eat,
Resistance assists a body and mind
In balance. Enzymes brandishing placards:
SUPER BUGS BEWARE! On the river of
Life, bone broth splashes both sides of the banks.
Where lies the détente in such sacred lands?
Diplomatic training requires one to
Circulate, bridging a unified peace.

Bamboozled

As I wrap my head around the sixty-
Year-old stalk, I lean in closer, placing
My ear against it. My hand easily
Glides along stacked foliage. The smoothness
Cool to the touch. I close my eyes, sensing
An inner vibration. "Hey, look at this!"
I shout out. I hear a rustling, and my
Friend emerges from a tangle of stalks.
The sensation of aluminum, spray-
Painted mint-green, is what I am wrapping
My head around. I follow it up to
The sky, beyond a canopy of thin
Pointed leaves. My friend hands me her phone, and
A game of hide-and-seek is captured on
Camera one frame at a time, blending
My friend's dark clothing with the darkened patches
Sewn into the stalks of yet another
Species. Turning in circles with open
Arms, spinning before us for all of the
World to see, is a forest of bamboo.
Giant slabs hang in a wind chime above
Us. Weathered stalks, tied with the twist of a
Knot, invite us to rest. In contrast, the
Cut stalks I'd seen in water-filled buckets
At nurseries had retained their luster.
Had I more than gazed upon these, in the
Grove today, I would not have been surprised,
Holding life in the hollow of a heart.

God. Source. All That Is.

As the breeze flows through the trees, I wonder
Where it began. It extends all the way
To where I now sit. Gaining strength, it lifts
The opposite page of my sketchbook as
I write. What on earth separates me from
This breeze? A lone bird flies by, coasts, and dips
Out of sight while the sweet songs of others
Spring forth through the leaves. Please answer me this:
God. Source. All That Is. Where may I find the
True beginning? At present, my inner
World is void of gusty winds. Elsewhere, a
Storm brews. Darkened clouds trail along the ridge.
Yet within, the clouds dissipate. Eyes closed,
God. Source. All That Is—it rains only peace.

PART TWO
The Art of War

The Promise of Peace

The blast threw me off of my feet.
As I rose, you fell to your knees.
My blood burns like flames on the street.
Shards of glass blind my eyes but I see.
Extended hand lay down your arms,
Three winters, four springs have gone by.
River of life spit out your charms,
Wash the tears that I no longer cry.
Fresh fallen snow covers torn leaves,
Moss weaves a carpet of fleece,
Smooth rounded stones, symphonic reprieve
From the source flows the promise of peace.
Voices call out: "The current is strong!"
Fill my lungs, Sarajevo, with song.

The Likes of Me

To ancient cultures I held out my hand.
Walled cities, desert, the ocean, the sea,
Beyond every mountain the promised land
Has welcomed with wonder the likes of me.
Cracked leather, charred heels, a hole in my boot,
Retracing my steps, I cannot find home,
In richness of soil where I take root
The world writ large I continue to roam.
Taking my leave as the crowd stumbles by,
I offer alms at the foot of the throne
A suitable boy, a latticework sky—
Will I love you more than life, save my own?
Beyond every mountain, waves from the sea,
Have welcomed with wonder the likes of me.

Blind Return

East crossing West at two rivers a crux
Rubble on curbsides torn windows and walls
Bleeding of hearts blind return left in flux—
From gleaming tips—Long Rod Bullets—life falls.
Turning back time with the skin of bare hands
Life is worth living although it is lost
Headstones on hillsides on still, fertile lands
Fruit of late harvests at double the cost.
Vapid, the sidewalks, death treading cement
Sky-colored canopies float on thin air
Pebbles on footsteps, a waltz of lament
Fingers stir foam in cracked cups as I stare.
Brandy in goblets, grilled kilos of meat,
Dried plums distilled from my tears bittersweet.

Christ Age Prague Spring

The striking clock calls out your time is near
Apostles pass as death rings out the bell
Christ-age Prague spring cloaks cobblestones in fear
Stark monuments share stories none shall tell.
To enter heaven upon golden wings
Pass under archways laden with God's stone
A child's cry deafens ears of lesser kings—
Closed lids, blank armor decorates the throne.
Crossbow in hand, we aim with knobby knees
We plead with Kafka eyes below the sill
Infant of Prague, please separate the seas,
Hold up thy head, avert the rains by will.
Atop the Charles Bridge raindrops chill the air
As Russian boots storm through the open square.

Thy Neighbor's Heart

The beauty of the sunlight leaves my eyes
As does the midnight moon—retreating.
Wide-eyed children knock stars down from the sky
With thy neighbor's heart, which has stopped beating.
After the shots had rung-out through the night,
The convoys arrived without incident—
Truckloads of rightful wares to ease the plight
Of a million plus souls, with prayers, were sent.
Thy neighbor has seen how life can laugh
In the faces of children, wielding sticks
And stones—war waged by angels on behalf
Of their mothers, whose spirits like…clocks…tick…
Justice lies dormant while souls stand pleading,
With thy neighbor's heart, which has stopped beating.

After the Conflict Before the Peace

After the conflict, before the peace, tell
Me—what is left of life when a beating heart
Is cut out of a chest—cleaving? Ripping
Back flesh, warm blood on your hands—eternal
Life or unsung death? At once you take flight,
Waning on a river, winding freely
Through deep-cut channels until, squinting—
You find yourself deposited safely
On the other side. Oh! The cool waters,
Warm sun waxing, spring emerges, marking
Time on the smoothest of stones—hard as nails,
Your soul once again filled with life. Without
Question you pick yourself up, content in
Knowing, this day—that, yes!—you are alive.

PART THREE
The Science of Illusion

The Test of Time

The calm before the storm, withstood well the
Test of time. Soon, the breaking waves will once
Again, barrel onto the shore. As they
Gather strength, I sit in wait, observing
As future unfolds. As sole witness, I
Watch as time pulls itself back to where it
Needs to be—to where it's always been—
The rub between finger and thumb. A spoof
Of the ageless. Indivisible. The
Spectrum of vibration in eight octaves.
A metronome sways, dancing in place as
Time conducts a chorus of northern lights.
From where has it come? To where will it go?
From moment to moment, does it exist?

Silent Music

Imagine a kiss being blown—
Words gone missing between the lines
The backside is all that is shown
As notes shed the skin of confines.
Leave me in peace to plod along
Beside the music of choices
Propelled by a burst void of song—
Space welcomes notable voices.
Closeness is but approximate
The silence is felt in my heart,
The sound of a lone predicate
Defines the vastness of my art.
Deaf, to the sunlight, still I stare
At that which is, and is not there.

Absolute Knowing

For the love of it. Write it. Recite it.
Believe. In liminal spaces one grasps
New ideas. Thoughts at our fingertips.
At ten to the negative thirty-three,
The music of compressed time. Our stories
In wait. Nothing can be more powerful,
Victor Hugo says. Creation at its
Best. Write what you know with confidence. As
If it were a calling. Ride alongside
A flash of light as far as time permits.
For the love of it. Write it. Recite it.
Believe. An inner voice trills, do you hear?
Absolute knowing resides in Planck's length.
Liminal spaces the advent of faith.

Fun with Physics

The delivery truck arrived and backed
Into my yard at a 90 degree
Angle. The logo painted on the truck
Read: *Fun with Physics*. A cut-out of a
Mini-explosion was applied under
The word "Boom!" A single atom dotted
The exclamation. The beeping stopped, and
The driver jumped out of the cab. He climbed
Up onto the trailer, unlatched the door
And it swung upon. Inside lay millions
Of multi-colored puzzle pieces. None
Were boxed. The driver pulled a shovel off
Of the trailer wall. Leaning on it, he
Asked, "Where would you like me to put these, Ma'am?"

Falling to Grace

So many are my guilty pleasures—vice
Underscores this life of mine. My very
Reality, biting down the bones. Self-
Redemption scours the depths of "now." Under-
Educated am I in the cloak of
Non-denominational consciousness.
Destiny unhinged. Purpose out of reach.
Electricity devoid of current.
Refraction in opposition to *Source*.
Time spinning pinwheels into a vacuum,
Oneness snaps open a ray of white light—
God-like in its command of energy.
Opulence as fine as a well-aged wine,
Deepest desire the vibration of love.

Three Standard Deviations

A man in his middle years sat with his
Father. When the waitress came, he handed
Her his card, and she swiped it on her pad.
"She's swiping all the cash from my account,"
He joked. Confused, his father reached for his
Cane, shifting from side-to-side to get out
Of the booth. The man returned with his young
Daughter the next day. He slipped her into
A booster chair. When the check came, they both
Reached out to grab it. The man nodded, and
The waitress smiled as the toddler smeared her
Sticky fingers on the signature line.
On the drive home, the man became lost in
His thoughts. A book he'd read as a child came
To mind. Antoine de Saint-Exupéry, a
Pilot, had written it. As a boy, the
Man had wanted to be a pilot, but
He'd pursued statistics. "The Little Prince"
Had taught him how to sum up the nature
Of reality. One small planet. One
Volcano. One rose bush, a glass cover
Placed on it for protection. Within the
Gullet of a boa constrictor, the
Whole of humanity—a bell curve. He,
An ordinary man, plotted near the
Median. Three standard deviations
From the mean—anomalies—his father
And his daughter, tails on opposite ends.

The Shadow of Power

Animal or mineral are counted
As material. The mass of planets
Fall into the bucket of measurement,
A mere statistic alongside height, weight,
The pressure of the air we breathe but may
Not hold. Mass is energy. Space is time,
In a rotating world that only the
Mind of science dare define. One side of
A silver-headed coin, whose currency,
Calculated to the nearest penny,
Accounts for information as if it
Were power. "Yes," I say. "But what of all
The other sides? The subtle sides? Does not
All exist in the shadow of power?"

The Great Halls of Science

As I stare at the pencil, eyes sharpened,
The pencil remains objectified. It
Does not float. Light does not dance a two-step
On either plane alongside that which my
Mind alone created. But, gazing in
Stillness with softened eyes, observation
Orchestrates the notes of each atom, in
Sync throughout space-time. This I do not grasp,
As once I had grasped the pencil. My mind's
Eye, witness to the mysteriousness
As consciousness gravitates back to lead.
If one mind can transform a pencil, what
Becomes of the "hard question" as many
Minds gaze into the great halls of science?

Double-blind Were We

Their battles waged beyond fear of science,
One might now say. The fear was that of man—
An unyielding, ill-curious sort. Rife
Once had made history, observing the
Center of a cancerous cell, nested
In a hierarchy of cells, each flush
With bacteria. Fractal in nature.
Spirals to infinity. Lost, are the
Frequencies once believed to heal. A cloud
Of ashes on an ocean of orgone.
If the microscopes developed by Rife
Had all not been smashed to smithereens, we
Might be able to see differently.
One man's intuition rests on a field
Of possibilities. A lifetime of
Memories only he can resurrect.
Meticulous research with promising
Findings (what are the odds?) make not a quack.
Reich gave us bodywork. His breath work fueled
The flames of his passion, as his own work
Went up in smoke. Tons of it! Banned were his
Reich boxes—destroyed by the FDA.
Rife took to the bottle. Imprisoned, Reich
Died. Both men consumed by a culture of
Ridicule, simply because it was not
Their time. The search for lost remedies, when
And if Found, warrant re-trial. The study,
When it is designed, will be double-blind.

The Power of Choice

A Nobel Prize! Al-Khalili says, for
He who can explain for us the two-split
Experiment. Leave the crested waves. Let
Go the grains of sand. The magic lies not
In an explanation for the masses.
Science will advance itself. There is no
Need for such a lofty goal, if the sole
Prize is merely recognition (and cash!).
The true pioneer seeks wellness that we
Can double in amplitude. By shifting
Our focus from outer perception to
Inner knowing, attention gives form to
Health. We have free will to choose. What do *you*
Want to be, a particle or a wave?

If Midnight Were Noon

If midnight were noon, birds would sleep with eyes
Wide open. Crickets would feather their wings.
Strings of sunlight would form a translucent
Tube around the moon. Consciousness would cloak
Our souls in dreams, if midnight were noon....
I awake to the gawking of a wild flock
Of birds. I peer through the blinds. Half the flock
Flutters in shattered symmetry.
The others rest, suspended on the leaves
Of a nearby tree. The break of dawn folds
The moon into a blanket of sunlight,
Awakening time. I lie back down and
Let shut my eyes. The birds coalesce, bond and
Move on, their wings tracing patterns of song.

Lodestar

A breath of hydrogen four hundred and
Eight light years from the earth. Pathfinder of
The waterways, guru of inner light,
Polaris is the retina of man.
Enchiridion of the soul, pages
Of discovery spread across the night
Sky. The broil of the infinite springs in
Shades of red from Ursa Minor. A stream
Of a trillion flames reabsorb the cast-
Away fumes of time, before reflecting
Them back through the lodestar. Stored data in
A vacuum. The energy of stardust,
Repurposed as luminous particles.
The fire of a photon, the whole of thought.

PART FOUR
Zero to Infinity

A Mother's Touch

I placed my palm on your shoulder and pressed
My middle finger into the blade. You
Coughed. My hands met in front of your heart. "Your
Mother is here." Her soul, rising up through
My toes. *I stand before you in grace.* I
Looked up at you in awe, wondering if
I should go on. My hands unfolded and
Reached out. *I handed you your daughter through
My fingertips.* The phrase, matter-of-fact.
I'm in the trees. I'm in the breeze…. I laughed,
Briefly cutting her off. "She's coming through
To you in a poem!" Your eyes said, go
On. *I want you to live with ease.* Around
You, I wrapped the arms of time. None, had passed.

Radio Flyer

To the precipice, I drag my wagon.
It's been with me since childhood, and although
I have out-grown it, the wagon retains
It's heavy load. By now, it's just a pile
Of mush, the weight of one human brain. Yet,
The matter still tugs at me after all
These years. I ask God to take it from me.
"I no longer want to drag this behind
Me," I tell him. The wagon lights up as
Bright as an eight-point star. As the handle
Drops from my hand, Orion bends down to
Pick it up, and the wheels roll into sky—
In search of Pleiades, where the mother star
Of the Milky Way with warm cookies waits.

A Stream of Grace

I chose you to be my conduit. You were
Wholly unaware at the time, but I
Knew exactly what you had decided.
What was best for you, indeed was also
The best you could do for me. I lingered.
Your measure of time, the weight of thirty-
Three years. As I had not yet learned to walk,
I rose into the otherworld. A wisp
Of indelibility. I had grown
Before I was born. As I sat with you
In your thoughts today, I saw through the eyes
Of time that you also had grown. The soft
Bell sounded as I spread my wings. A lone
Jet in the ether, absconding in grace.

Future Perfect

"Meet me in the plasma. I'll wait for you
There." I take a deep breath and George appears.
He came to me as a white butterfly
When I was in Africa. "Hi, George!" I'd
Say as he fluttered by. He tells me there
Will be more parties. He says there will be
Many. My heart drops back to a time when
We were young. Before I left the U.S.
Before he was gone. It does no good to
Argue. He trumps me every time. "You have
More work to do than I did," he laughs. That
Wonderful, warm, heartfelt laugh. "Oh, right," I
Say. Another party must be starting—
A butterfly dips by and disappears.

Fight or Flight

Can you hear the birds as they flap their wings?
This is me as the color of sky. When
You are blue, in a *whoosh* I am gone. I
Didn't think you would miss me when you have
Other subtle bodies that you attend
To each day. I prefer not to stay home;
It's so much easier to take flight. I
Have more fun with Casper, the friendly ghost.
With him and the others I play—stretching
My tether to the thinnest possible
Strand of light before I snap and jolt
You back into the present. Then I go
Back out again. But make me a home filled
With love, and in a heartbeat, I will stay.

White Light

I pick up the rose quartz and hold it close
To my heart. "White light, white light, white light," I
Say aloud. Then I drape myself in an
Additional layer of green, healing
Light. Some say if you protect yourself with
Light, you acknowledge that dark energies
Exist. Better safe than sorry, I think
As I grab my keys. I start the engine
And back out of the drive. Once on the road,
"White light, white light, white light," I say aloud,
"That all I pass be filled with light, and that
Which lies ahead." I thank all of my guides,
But keep my hands tight on the wheel at ten
And two, in case I drive under a cloud.

When Spirit Calls

The light turned red as I neared the corner.
I put on my turn signal and waited.
I felt a nudge and heard a thought: *Drive one
More block.* I ignored it. I was nearly
Home. The thought became more persistent: *Drive!*
As the light turned green, my car rolled forward,
The wheel now firmly in my hands.
I parked next to the side entrance,
Under the dome. But for the choir on the
Alter, the Basilica was empty.
In her hand, the Virgin held a single
Lily. Votives flickered at her feet. As
I dropped down on my knees, the choir sang out:
"Lord, make me an instrument of your peace."

Ascended Development

Francis Banks lived well on this earth. She was
At best, insatiable. No matter
How much knowledge she soaked up, she was left
Pinning for more. At times, experience
Alluded her. In comparison, all
Else paled before her physical eyes. Oh!
How much more clearly she came to see on
The other side. She worked in a transit
Center. This is where she understood the
Self as purveyor of illusion. Her
Concept of reality sharpened. She
Continued with her unending pursuit
Of *knowing* as the many layers of
Her soul were unleashed. At the center? Light.

EPILOGUE
Sonnet Cycle of the Seven Chakras

1. Muladhara (The Root Chakra)

Closing my eyes, as angels stand guard, I
Fall quickly and quietly toward the earth.
As I descend singularity, my
Vibration gains density. With a slap,
I am born. Swaddled in a field of dreams
I take my first breath, grasping Gaia's slim
Fingers as gravity lays me down. I
Sense my existence and let go a yelp.
Primal feelings lace my memories in
A delicate shroud. Forgotten not have
I from whence I have come. Still, I am stunned.
Anodea Judith says, to find our
Form, we need only look toward our ground. I
Stare back in wonder. My search has begun.

2. Svadhisthana (The Dwelling Place of Self)

Seat of sexuality, element
Of water. Release and containment in
Equal measure. An effortless movement.
Locomotion of emotion as the
Lotus unfolds one petal at a time.
Too many at once excessive, too few
Less divine. United is the whole of
Individuation. Creation of
A "fuzzy logic" beyond zeroes and
Ones. In the center of the ocean one
Finds the outlines of the soul, six-petaled.
"Soul," an individual expression
Of spirit. "Spirit," the universal
Expression of self. Sensual in form.

3. Manipura (City of Gems)

The warmth of sensuality rises
From below. At the center of the sun,
Success shines brightly. Doubt yourself not here.
The power of your will resides in "clear
Sensing" within fields of information.
Rise above it, and you will fall in love.
The base of spirituality thrives
When energy flows downward before it
Reaches back up, defying gravity.
Don't be fooled, no matter how deep the wounds.
To heal them, movement and emotion are
Essential elements. Trust. Let go as
"The natural healing process takes place
Under the bandage."[3] Honor your power.

4. Anahata (The Heart Chakra)

As the Father of creation holds out
His hand, within his fist the heart of a
Woman is transformed. Conscious unity
In perfect balance. The healing of the
Sacred revolves here. To heal the heart is
To heal the whole of the subtle world. The
Color of nature the language of love.
The twelve-petaled lotus teaches us well:
To keep our ego in check, step with our
Shadow into the light, nurture both sides
Of our soul. At the center, sparked by the
Union of heaven and earth, resides the
Divine. Anima/animus. A child,
Knowing she is enough just as she is.

5. Vishuddha (Purification)

As the surrounding earth vibrates, blue light
Dances as the storyteller chants. The
Sense of timing is impeccable. All
Within listening range are enraptured.
"I share with you what springs from the bottom
Of my heart," we are told. One can also
Find balance in affirmations. "I hear
And speak the truth. I express myself with
Clear intent. Creativity flows in
And through me," Anodea Judith said.
"My voice is necessary." Yet, many
Shy away from what needs most to be said.
Give voice to your thoughts. Soundwaves double in
Amplitude when combined, creating strength.

6. Anja (Perception and Self-Realization)

Beyond the imagination is the
Song of symbols. Patterns of perception
Drawn from the base of our identify.
Behind the curtain of the unconscious
One finds not a pile of rubbish, Jung said.
This is where our individual lives
Are determined in invisible ways.
Through intuition, one gains an enhanced
Awareness of oneself. False impressions
Dissolve. With our full potential in view,
We are free to form our own mandalas.
We manifest ourselves through this chakra,
Creating, in Dale's words: *a stream of grace.*[4]
Before our own eyes, consciousness takes shape.

7. Sahasrara (The Crown Chakra)

How is it, I wonder, that the world can
Contain such iridescence? How is it
That energy pulsates from the deepest
Throes of the cosmos to the center of
My soul? Ever present. Defying space
And time. A lightness of being void of
Mass. Free of words. Except one. Love. As we
Develop within the circle of life,
Within our own microcosmic orbit,
We breathe. At our crown, we both receive and
Release. With bodies firmly planted, we
Are free to raise our hearts and transcend. The
Shimmer of pileum graces sky. As
The flock approaches, I spread out my wings.

Author's Note: In the ancient Vedic tradition, chakras are subtle energy centers. There are seven main chakras: 1) the root, 2) the sacral, 3) the solar plexus, 4) the heart, 5) the throat, 6) the third eye, and 7) the crown. The chakras are aligned with the anatomy of the brain and the spine. These energy centers are also energetically connected to various systems in the body such as the plexuses, endocrine, and nervous systems. The chakras are also associated with colors, sounds, and symbols.

ABOUT THE AUTHOR

Julie R. Dargis spent many years working internationally, supporting refugees and local communities affected by war and natural disasters. Her first book, *Pit Stop in the Paris of Africa* (2013), is a collection of narrative essays and verse highlighting her work overseas. She is also author of *White Moon in a Powder Blue Sky* (2016), a volume of poetry and prose exploring the nature of consciousness.

A member of the Association of Comprehensive Energy Psychology (ACEP), the Consciousness Healing Initiative (CHI), and the Poetry Society of America, Dargis resides in Carlsbad, California, where she is currently pursuing a PhD in integral health at the California Institute for Human Science, a research facility dedicated to the mind-body-spirit connection.

For more information, visit:
www.juliedargis.com

ENDNOTES

1. Hiroshi Motoyama & Rande Brown, *Science and the Evolution of Consciousness: Chakras, Ki and Psi,* (Brookline: Autumn Press, 1978), 138.

2. Matthieu Ricard & Trinh Xuan Thuan, *The Quantum and the Lotus,* (New York: Three Rivers Press, 2001), *63*.

3. Anodea Judith, *Eastern Body, Western Mind: Psychology of the Chakra System as a Path to Self,* (Berkeley: Celestial Arts, 2004), 151.

4. Cyndi Dale, *The Subtle Body Practice Manual: A Comprehensive Guide to Energy Healing,* (Boulder: Sounds True, 2013), 105.

FURTHER READING

Healing and the Subtle Body

Dale, Cyndi. *The Subtle Body: An Encyclopedia of Your Energetic Anatomy.* Boulder: Sounds True, 2009.

Dispenza, Joe. *You are the Placebo: Making Your Mind Matter.* Carlsbad: Hay House, 2014.

Dossey, Larry. *One Mind: How Our Individual Mind is Part of a Greater Consciousness and Why it Matters.* Carlsbad: Hay House, 2013.

Eden, Donna with Feinstein, David. *Energy Medicine: Balancing Your Body's Energies for Optimal Health, Joy, and Vitality.* New York: Jeremy P. Tarcher/Penguin, 2008.

Gerber, Richard. *Vibrational Medicine: A Practical Guide to Energy Healing and Spiritual Transformation.* New York: William Morrow, 2001.

Goswami, Amit. *The Quantum Doctor: A Physicist's Guide to Health and Healing.* Charlottesville: Hampton Roads, 2004.

Judith, Anodea. *Eastern Body Western Mind: Psychology and the Chakra System as a Path to the Self* (Revised). Berkeley: Celestial Arts, 2004.

Motoyama, Hiroshi & Brown, Rande. *Science and the Evolution of Consciousness: Chakras, Ki, and Psi.* Brookline: Autumn Press, 1978.

Pert, Candace. *Molecules of Emotion: The Science of Mind-body Medicine.* New York: Scribner, 1997.

Targ, Russell & Katra, Jane. *Miracles of Mind: Exploring Nonlocal Consciousness and Spiritual Healing.* Novato: New World Library, 1999.

Van Der Kolk, Bessel. *The Body Keeps the Score: Brain, Mind, and Body in the Healing of Trauma.* New York: Penguin, 2014.

Intuition and the Soul

Bodine, Echo. *A Still, Small Voice: A Psychic's Guide to Awakening Intuition.* Novato: New World Library, 2001.

Roberts, Jane. *Seth Speaks: The Eternal Validity of the Soul.* San Rafael: Amber-Allen Publishing, 1994.

Singer, Michael. *The Untethered Soul: The Journey Beyond Yourself.* Oakland: Noetic Books, 2007.

Physics and the Nature of Reality

Dalai Lama XIV. *The Universe in a Single Atom: The Convergence of Science and Spirituality.* New York: Harmony, 2006.

Einstein, Albert. *Relativity: The Special & the General Theory, 100th Anniversary Edition.* Princeton: Princeton University Press, 2015.

Greene, Brian. *The Elegant Universe: Superstrings, Hidden Dimensions, and the Quest for the Ultimate Theory.* New York: W. W. Norton, 2010.

Ho, Mae-Wan. *The Rainbow and the Worm: The Physics of Organisms.* Singapore: World Scientific, 2008.

Lipton, Bruce H. *The Biology of Belief: Unleashing the Power of Consciousness, Matter & Miracles.* Carlsbad: Hay House, 2008.

Ricard, Matthieu & Xuan Thuan, Trinh. *The Quantum and the Lotus: A Journey to the Frontiers where Science and Buddhism Meet.* New York: Three Rivers Press, 2001.

McTaggart, Lynne. *The Field: The Quest for the Secret Force of the Universe.* New York: Harper, 2008.

Radin, Dean. *The Conscious Universe: The Scientific Truth of the Psychic Phenomena.* New York: Harper Collins, 1997.

Rosenblum, Bruce & Kuttner, Fred. *Quantum Enigma: Physics Encounters Consciousness* (Second Edition). Oxford: Oxford University Press, 2001.

Sheldrake, Rupert. *Science Set Free: 10 Paths to New Discovery.* New York: Random House, 2012.

Talbot, Michael. *The Holographic Universe.* New York: Harper Perennial, 1992.

Zukov, Gary. *The Dancing Wu Li Masters: An Overview of the New Physics.* New York: William Morrow, 1979.

The Afterlife and Near-Death Experiences

Alexander, Eben. *Proof of Heaven.* New York: Simon and Schuster, 2012.

Bodine, Echo. *Echoes of the Soul: The Soul's Journey Beyond the Light through Life, Death, and Life After Death.* Novato: New World Library, 1999.

Greaves, Helen. *Testimony of Light: An Extraordinary Message of Life After Death.* New York: Jeremy P. Tarcher/Penguin, 1969.

Moody, Raymond A. *Life After Life.* New York: HarperOne, 1975.

Moorjani, Anita. *Dying to Be Me: My Journey from Cancer, to Near Death, to True Healing.* Carlsbad: Hay House, 2012.

Tucker, Jim B. *Return to Life: Extraordinary Cases of Children Who Remember Past Lives.* New York: St. Martin's Press, 2015.

Weiss, Brian L. *Many Lives, Many Masters: A True Story of a Prominent Psychiatrist, His Young Patient, and the Past-Life Therapy that Changed Both Their Lives.* New York: Touchstone, 1988.

www.ingramcontent.com/pod-product-compliance
Lightning Source LLC
Chambersburg PA
CBHW072026060426
42449CB00035B/2879